THE CHARLIE BROWN COLLECTION™

ISBN 978-0-634-03098-7

HAL•LEONARD®

Visit Hal Leonard Online at
www.halleonard.com

CONTENTS

Charlie Brown Theme

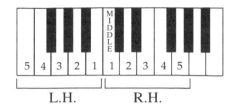

By Vince Guaraldi

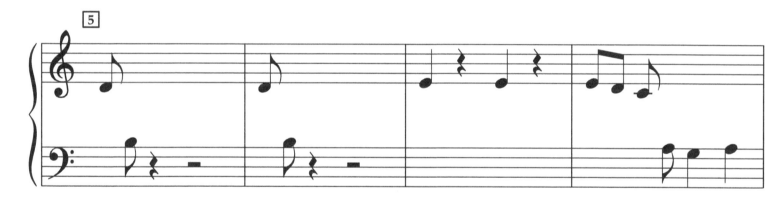

Duet Part (Student plays one octave higher than written.)

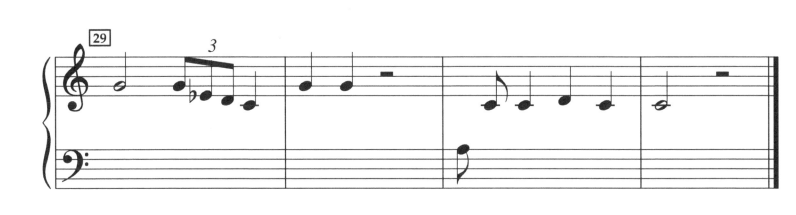

Christmas Time Is Here

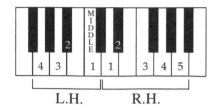

L.H.   R.H.

Words by Lee Mendelson
Music by Vince Guaraldi

Christ-mas time   is   here,   hap - pi - ness   and   cheer.
Snow-flakes in   the   air,   car - ols ev – 'ry - where.

Duet Part (Student plays one octave higher than written.)

Fun for all that chil-dren call their fa-v'rite time of year.
Old-en times and an-cient rhymes of love and dreams to

share. Sleigh-bells in the air, beau - ty ev - 'ry -

where. Yule-tide by the fire - side and joy - ful mem - 'ries

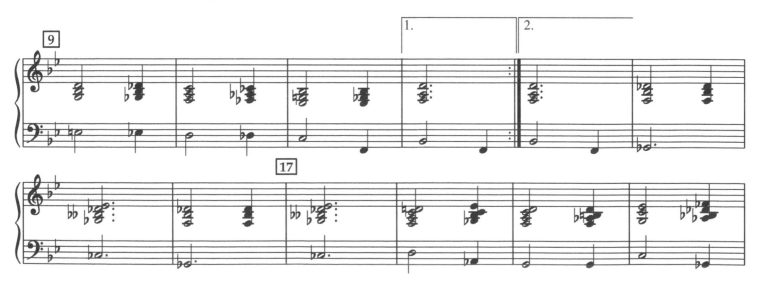

there. Christ-mas time is here,

we'll be draw – ing near. Oh, that we could

al – ways see such spir - it through the year.

(3)

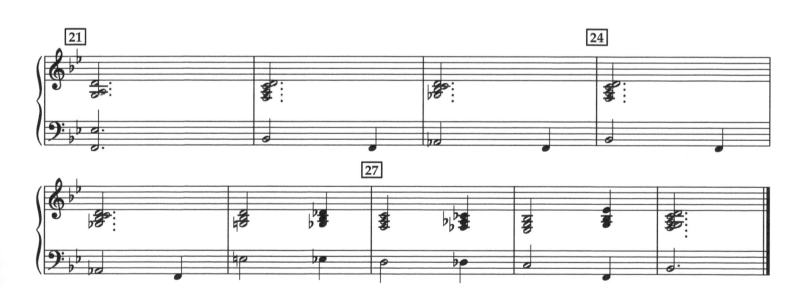

The Great Pumpkin Waltz

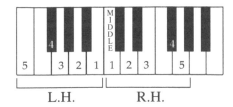

L.H.   R.H.

By Vince Guaraldi

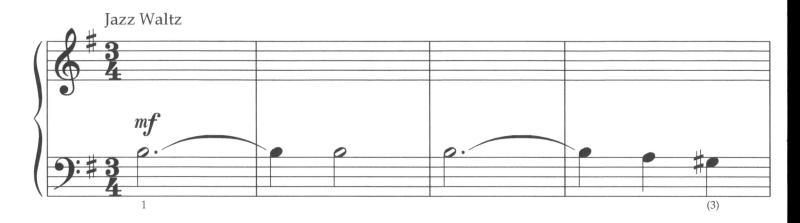

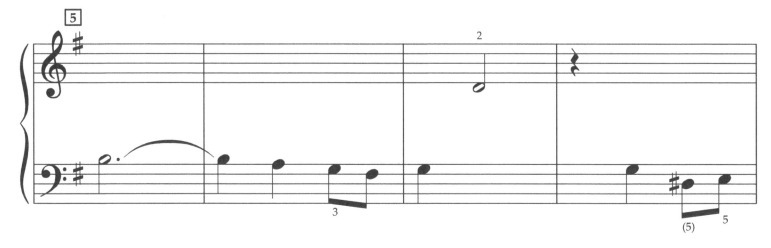

Duet Part (Student plays one octave higher than written.)

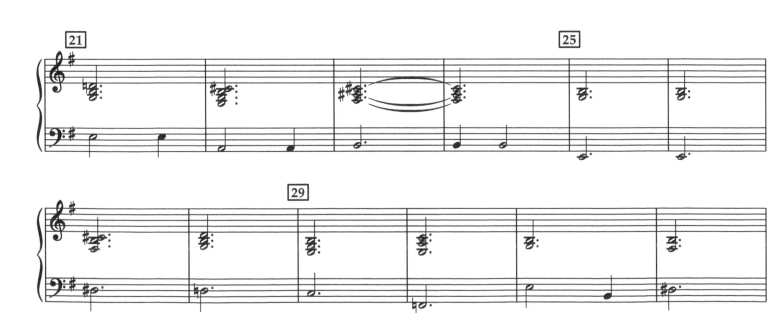

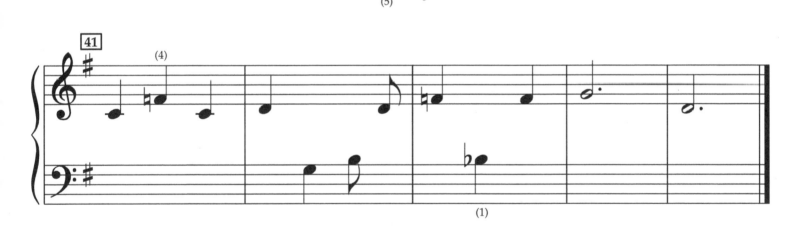

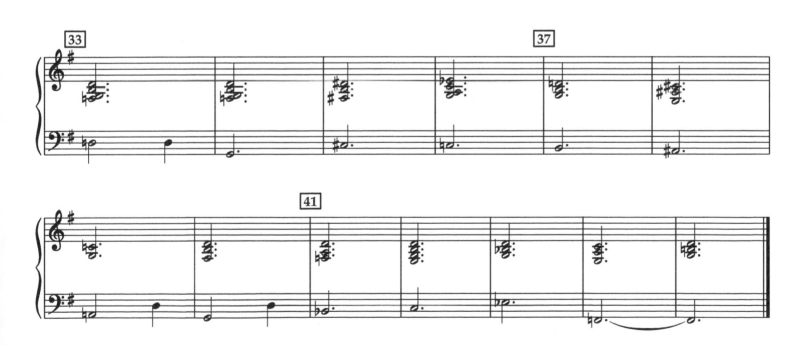

Linus and Lucy

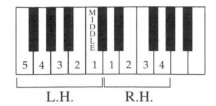

By Vince Guaraldi

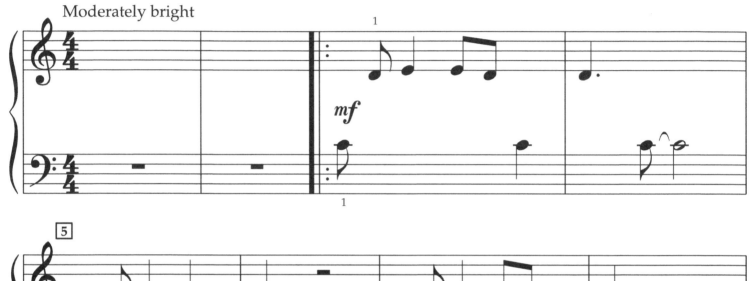

Duet Part (Student plays one octave higher than written.)

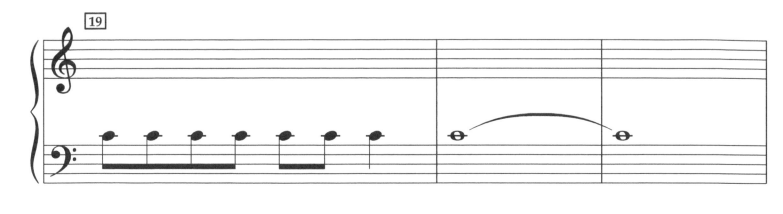

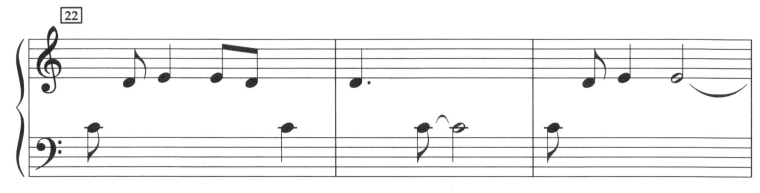

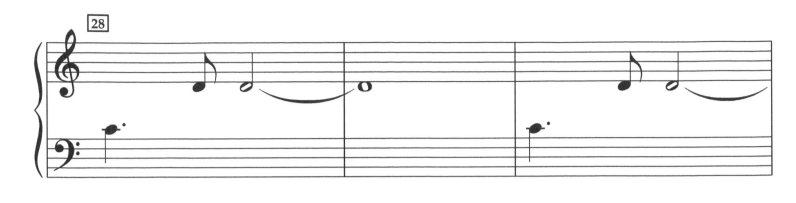

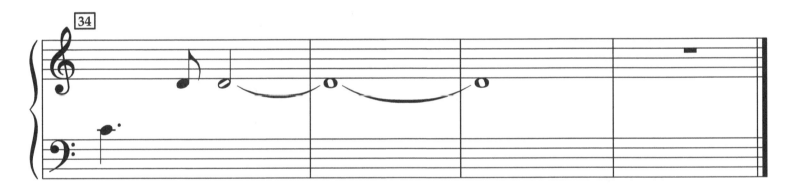

Oh, Good Grief

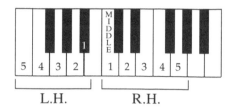

L.H.   R.H.

By Vince Guaraldi

Moderately

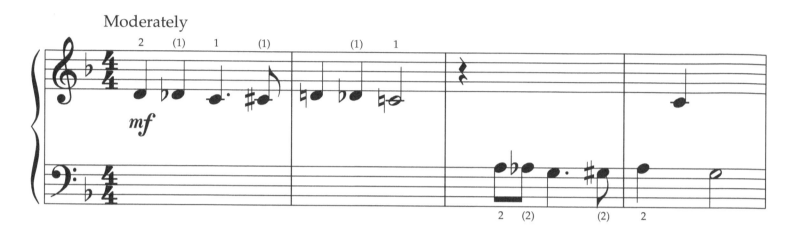

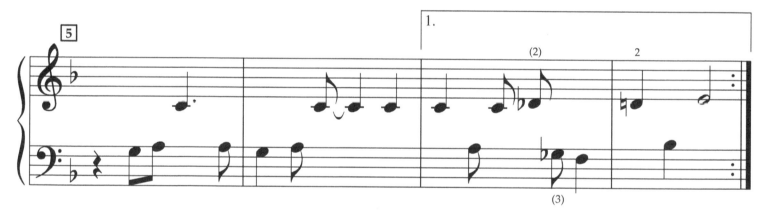

Duet Part (Student plays one octave higher than written.)

Moderately

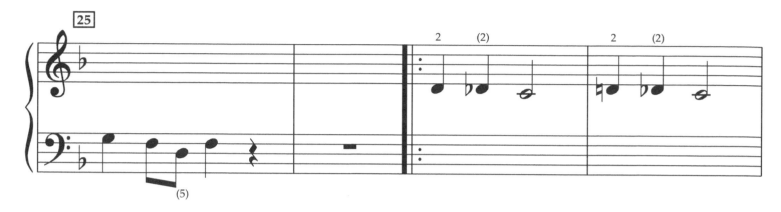

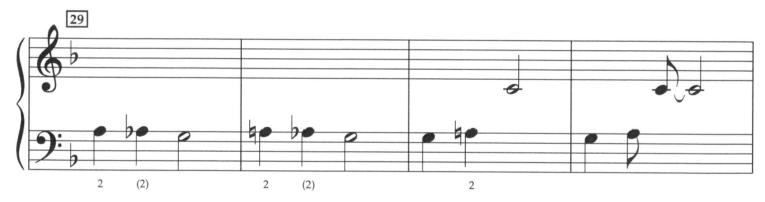

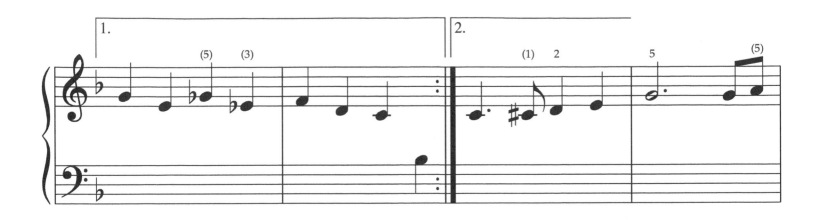

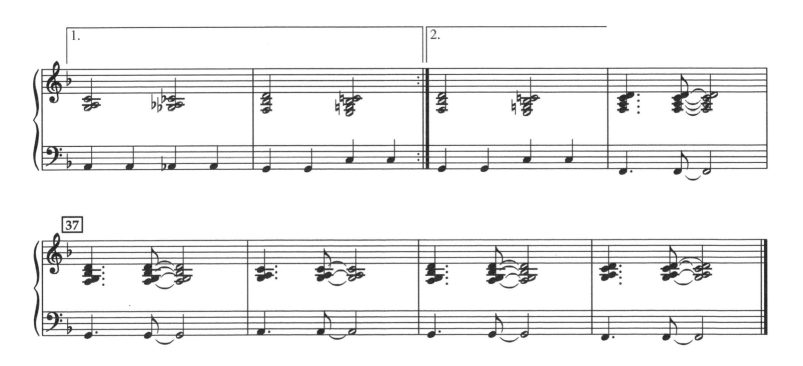

Schroeder

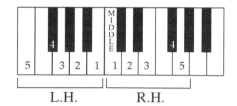

By Vince Guaraldi

Moderately

Duet Part (Student plays one octave higher than written.)
Moderately

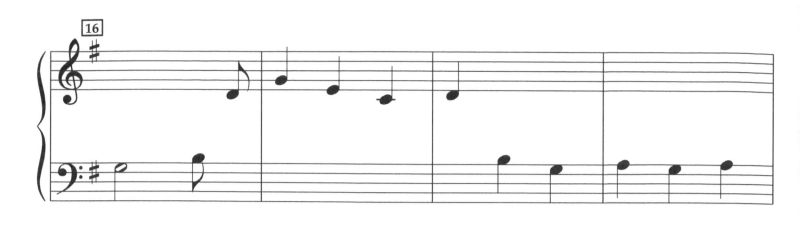

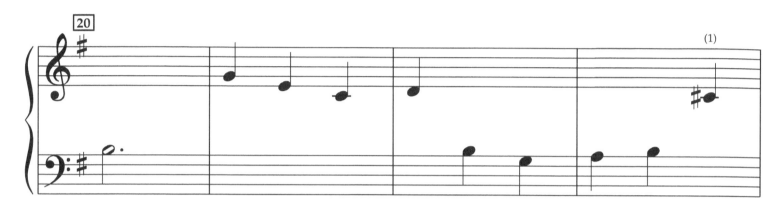

24

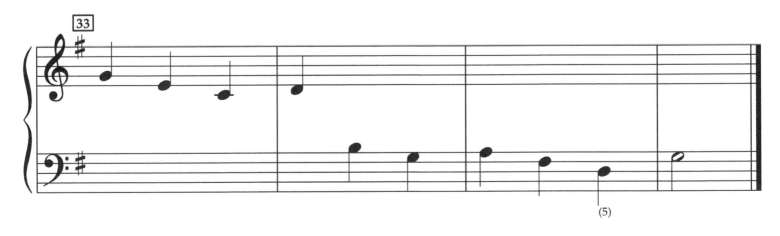

Skating

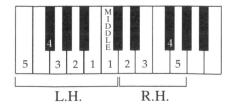

By Vince Guaraldi

Bright Jazz Waltz

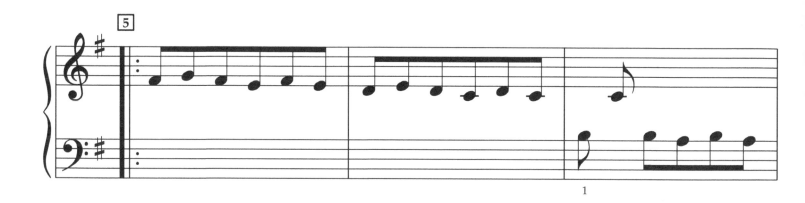

Duet Part (Student plays one octave higher than written.)

Bright Jazz Waltz

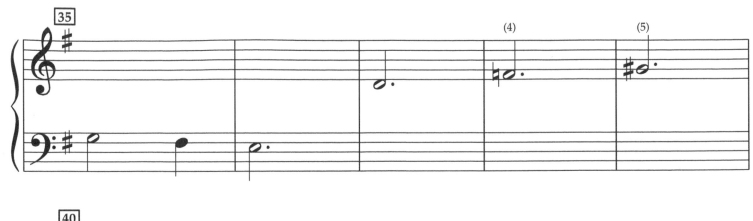

Love Will Come

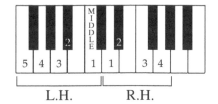

By Vince Guaraldi

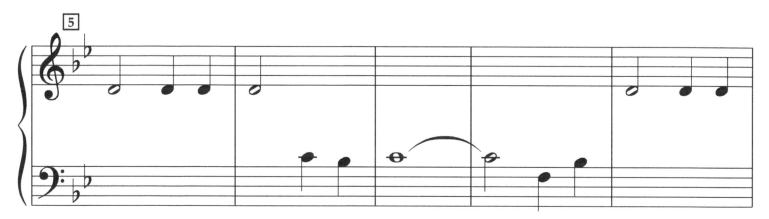

Duet Part (Student plays one octave higher than written.)

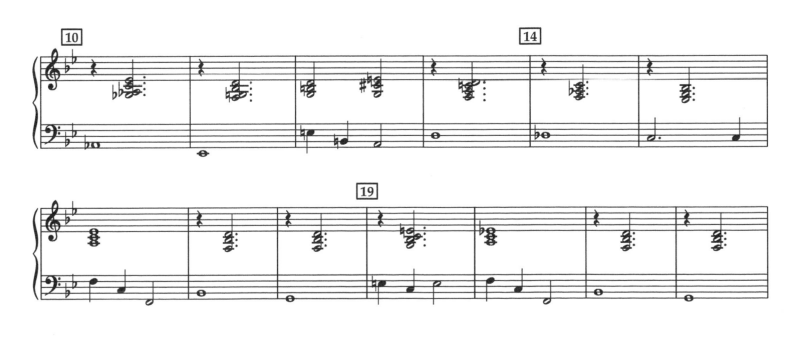

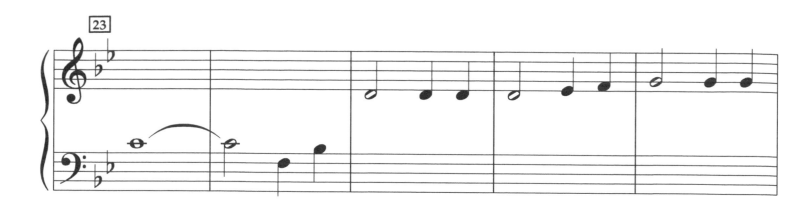